DEDICATION

For my wife, Mamasu
&
For the people of the Republic of Liberia.

.

CONTENTS

Acknowledgements

It is to GOD that I give the ultimate glory for without him this book and all other things in my life would not be possible.

Next, I am indebted infinitely to my gorgeous and always understanding wife, Mamasu, for being the glue that holds our family together while I spend countless hours engaging in this labor of love, this passion of mine: writing.

To the following professors: Althea Romeo-Mark, Dr. Patricia Jabbeh-Wesley, Dr. Celestine Kasasa, Dr. Leslie Levin, Marie McKay, Leticia Balajadia, and the late John S. Varflay, Jr. for teaching me the basics of the fine art of writing those many years ago when I lacked confidence in my own abilities, I extend my deepest gratitude.

To D. Othniel Forte, at **FORTE** Publishing, for his invaluable editing effort and for bringing the poems to life, I am beholden.

Finally, to all of my children: Momoh, Jr., Simita, Moinjama, Moinduana, Lucine, Sekou, and Makessa Akweleyvie, I am profoundly indebted. You all are the reason I do what I do and you each inspire me greatly in your own ways.

Author's Note

After nearly two decades away, I returned home to Liberia in March of 2016. As you may imagine, I was a cannon ball of excitement. There was a lot I looked forward to. I itched to catch up on lost time with family and friends as well as with the country itself.

On arrival, I wasted little time immersing fully in just about everything. There were the unending family gatherings, the late night conversations with Pops, unexpected reunions with friends of old, visitations to places of childhood memory, meetings with political leaders, radio show appearances, and much more. The experience of these re-acquaintances informs much of my ruminations in this collection.

If, for any reason, you find some of my interpretations of conditions in Liberia and elsewhere wanting, please understand they are but one man's unvarnished opinion of how things were at a point in time.

I wish you a very happy reading!

Momoh Sekou Dudu
Otsego, Minnesota
U.S.A.

Home Again

The plane descends
    hugging the rugged airstrip
    with but a few flickers-
        lighting the pitch-black runway!
My heart races!
        Not of fear or anxiety
        But from a forceful brew
        Of excitement
    Alas! I am home again

In the decades since I left,
    I played out this moment,
    repeatedly in my head!
    Now that it's finally here,
    I am unable to self-control
Oh! I am home again

        I disembark to a punishing swelter
        that threatens to suffocate me.
A bile rises in my throat,
        as a barrage of voices assault me
'Welcome Home!' they scream!
        but I refuse to get distracted
Because I am home again

Tears in 208

Yesterday in room 208,
    I cried.
My tears flowed unrestrained.
Tears of joy they were,
bitter tears of sorrow too,
they could have been.

    My eyes bawled, my heart hurt.
For a friend.
A friend for whom life was being altered,
yet restored.

Yesterday in room 208,
    I harbored mixed emotions;
    sadness and happiness all at once,
    longing for what I may not have told.

I offered prayers for a redo,
a chance for a new start.
I dreamt sweet dreams and bitter dreams,
Profound dreams they were.
but most of all,
    I cried......

Yesterday, in room 208,
    text messages flew everywhere,
they begged for answers;
"Any idea yet? I am anxious, I am sacred"
they mostly said.

In terse but hopeful responses,
the answers came to console me;
    "Progress" one flashed across my screen,
    whereupon I sat to wait some more.

The hours came and went,
so another text went begging,
as I put on a brave face,
to sit and await the next signal.
When that signal finally came,
    I shed some more bitter tears;
    for one thing was now abundantly clear:
    for my friend, the road ahead was still long.

Twisted Elites

Oh! Why so twisted
      Callous and gullible?
      Driving shiny, new motors
      On limited, dusty, patchy roads
      Comfortable in luxury
Yet, hiding behind tinted glasses

Oh why so daring?
      Going past the masses
      As they toil on empty bellies?
      Fetching for a survival so hard to garner?
      Ignoring those from whom they took
      Chances. Opportunities. Everything.
Now they clutch at droplets
we let slip through our fingers.

Oh! Why are we so self-seeking
    And impassive and amoral?
    That we live behind tall fences
    In the affluence of mansions
    Built on the blood and sweat and tears
    Of the suffering people?

        Yet, ignoring their cries, their pains
    Disregarding their losses, their deaths
            Why not stop and think
            And ask for once, why?
            Why the indifference

        To the plight of the people?
        Why live plush in their misery?
      Gosh! Some coldhearted elites....

Whole Again?

This village is not lost,
for somethings still work.
Even if they seem insignificant,
I rather them to the alternative
of the recent past.

I was here when the system failed;
a failure so brutal, so complete,
no mortal would have ever thought,
the things that work now, would ever do.

Do we not treasure the prevailing peace?
The fact we can say what we want?
Even if it's about the village chief?
That freedom, we should all cherish.

I know there are issues unresolved:
the roads, the schools, the hospitals
electricity, jobs, and even water.
Those things too will become whole again

So to thee deserving people,
I have for you a solemn plea:
To make the unresolved whole again,
entrust the village to sober minds.

Sunset Over Snail Hill

Something angelic hung
over Snail Hill. Suspended
on the sprawling horizon
of our field of a thousand cash crops

It wasn't hard to notice
for it was something special.
It held a hypnotic splendor
Beauty queens would die to possess

Just as I stood to ponder
A flock of rice birds flew by
Creating a colorful pattern
Across the pleasing vista

Beyond the creatures,
I saw the enchanted phenomenon
in its red and orange majesty.
It was the Sunset over Snail Hill

The Miseducation of Bigboy

Even in your laughter
I hear your solemn cries
Even when you smile,
I get a troubling message
Beneath it all; a message of
Heartbreak, of pain over
The systemic problem
Of the miseducation of Bigboy

When chastised for failing,
At an alarming rate,
That dreaded admissions exam
I understand that your troubles
Do not originate at your feet
But at the doorsteps of the system
A system responsible for
The miseducation of Bigboy

When you write
'where' for 'were'
or 'hear' for 'here'
I die inside for you.
It's not your fault,
for you are but a mirror
of the system that caused
the miseducation of Bigboy.

The next time you write
and it's filled with errors,
understand that you ain't
the culprit in this miseducation.
For it could have been different
were it not for the broken system
that gave you no foundation.
Thus, your miseducation Bigboy.

Hell's Traffic

Tension runs high
on the baking pavement
as angry men point fingers
in each other's faces
and trade vulgarities
that no one should have to utter.
Brought on, nonetheless,
by the fury of hell's traffic.

It is just past dusk
but that does not matter
as panic sets in and men—
seized by bluster—
explode as fiery fuel
in hell's damning traffic.

Northbound vehicles
Slowly head south
Stalling. Creeping. Inching

Oops! They face resistance
from southbound motors
determined to head north
and in that fog of hell's traffic,
chaos consumes them all.

To relieve the tension,
amidst all the confusion,
they start to zigzag.
Some heading eastward
While others head westward.

None minded that east and west
weren't meant for motors. Thus,
prolonging to eternity
our time in hell's traffic.

River of Life

Growing up in the quaint village,
in the foothills of the sacred mountains,
nature runs undisturbed;
spread out in its vast splendor.

A certain river flowed smoothly.
Its sanguine waters snaking over
a bed of white gravel;
serving in its curling path,
all lifeforms that yearned to live.

Of great importance is this river.
For I clearly recall how whenever
we crossed its vast expanse,
to and from the nourishing fields,
Momma failed never to remind me,
that it was the river of life.

We'd be nothing without it.
It provided us so much for so long-
food, water to drink, cleanser, etc.
thus, leaving me not a single doubt,
that it was indeed the river of life.

So even now from a 1000 miles away,
I fail never to sing the praise
of that rumbling waterway;
for unquestionably, it was the river of life.

Child Soldier

You of placid demeanor
Before you were robbed
Of your youth,
Your innocence,
Of your chance to grow up;
I hold no grudge towards you,
'Cus you were a mere child.

You of soft spoken words
Before your exploitation,
Were but a victim
To evil schemes of warlords
And their illicit drugs
I hold for you no rancor
'Cus you're but a lost child.

You of gentle mind
Before you were corrupted
By memories of vile deeds
And images of things you
Should have never seen,
I hold for you no blame
'Cus you're truly innocent.

You of stolen dreams,
Of futures brutally annulled,
Was no less a victim than was I
Of the war mongers' transgressions
Oh child, I ask for you salvation
As I do for me
'Cus we were but pawns
In the power games of perverted minds

Crossing to Safety

The Makona* thundered,
Screaming in vehement protest
Under the weight of
Troubled strangers
The exodus pressed on
Ignoring the river's dissent
Edging ever closer
To the zone of danger

There were crocs lurking
And other potential hazards
The migrants didn't hold back
For they had heard the dirges
of the 'brave' souls
Who'd chosen to stake a claim

As the river hollered
The march to safety continued
onward, across the waterway
they moved far away from the
evil forces whose only mission
Was to have them murdered

*The river that forms the boundary between the republics of
Sierra Leone and Guinea in West Africa.

Nearly Departed

He of vaunted repute
Remembered for vigor and oomph
Now lays with eyes unblinking
Weak and grizzled

How dare you father time?
Why impose such reckoning
On this humble soul
Who fought and endured?

He longs to hear and to see
He strains to ensure this comes to pass
But there is no denying
Times have changed
For when he now commands,
His ears and eyes refuse to oblige

Oh you gentle soul,
Once so buoyant, now so downcast
As you near your time appointed,
I find it impossible to say goodbye
Should you depart before I return
Know this: you're my hero eternal.

First Born Son

Soon upon my admittance,
the wise one voiced to me,
it wasn't a mistake, after all,
that I was the first to be called upon.

God, you see so,
the wise one confided in me,
sent you before the rest,
to prepare the way for them all.

Being the first born,
the wise one counseled me,
this comes with duties
you must be prepared to undertake.

It never matters even if,
the wise one cautioned me,
that he's in the wrong,
or that you're in the right.

That is why God remembered,
the wise one declared to me,
to bless you with a temperament,
that is as even keeled as it could be.

Go out therefore,
the wise one instructed me,
and spread peace offerings,
to the litany of your siblings.

Forgetting never to realize,
the wise one stressed to me,
that you are of all things,
the first born son.

From then onwards
I took a solemn pledge
to ignore the grievances I'd ever had and
become the 'first born' I was meant to be!

The Reason I Teach

I often ponder why I teach,
because I know it's not for the cash;
you're quite aware it couldn't be,
for teachers are among the least waged.

When I ponder this deeply,
I begin to figure out why I teach.
I teach because I'm passionate
to cultivate, to lead, to instigate
the young minds readying to takeover
tomorrow's affairs of our endangered world.

Already I have seen the grander good,
my years of teaching have birthed;
they come to the fore in varying forms:
from preachers, politicians and policemen
to merchants, teachers and artisans.

Each time a former pupil of mine,
becomes a force for the public good,
I melt with pride and great relief;
because of such little things,
I pledge my life to the teaching field.
I pledge to be a lifelong educator

Someday I may choose to do other things,
because life is such a marathon;
but I know for certain whatever I do,
I'd forever be a teacher at my core.

Not a Prisoner of my Mind

From cradle to grave,
I'd like to be the master;
not an indentured servant
to all the complexities;
Complexities buried
in my mind's deepest crevices.

You see,
In the depths of my mind,
lies a trove of treasure;
but equally compelling
therein, lies something else-
a hoard of burden.

Confused; cautious;
I thread ever carefully,
taking pains to not transform
into a prisoner of my mind.
Whenever needed,
I do retrieve the treasures.
But when I do so,
I often face a challenge
to ensure the burden remains buried;
for if it were to spring forth,
you'd call me crazy.

I Still Am

Like an unexpected blow,
swift, pulverizing, crushing me,
you explode into my ribs.
But haymaker, you're wrong about me!
For, in spite of that, I still stand!

Like a sandstorm,
intense, obstructive, blinding me,
you clutter my eyes.
But haymaker, you're mistaken about me!
For despite that, I still stand!

Like a virulent disease,
deadly, tiring, almost killing me
without pity, you infect.
But haymaker, ye know not what I'm made of!
For even with your enmity, I still breathe.

Here's what ye know not;
I am made of African clay,
resilient, unyielding to a haymaker's fury.
Thus, of clear vision, I still stand!
And I still breathe!

Melee at Redlight

His solitary eyes raged with fear
as he looked up toward the clenched fists
barreling down upon him
in a fit of anger;
he tried to run but found no path
for he was trapped in place
by a human barrier
that suffocated the market district;
it was a melee at Redlight.

His countenance was an amalgam of despair
as excited men and women cheered loudly
the crushing sound of colliding fists
fracturing his bony frame.
Overmatched,
he seized a beer bottle and swung wildly
in futile hopes of ending the bully's assault
inviting an even greater flurry of punches
upon his already battered body.
It was a melee at Redlight.

Heart of a Dandelion

So what do you think you are?
Some treatment-resistant staph?
Only fading but never gone?
I come after you so often,
with all the might I can call upon,
pumping in your veins, with great belief,
toxic potions of imminent death.

Thinking you'd be gone for eternity,
I become complacent and cocksure,
only to realize in time to come,
you're back from the dead with zestful glee,
proving to all that that heart of yours,
is genuinely of a dandelion.

I have poured so much into conquering you,
I have no idea what I must do next;
like the proverbial 'nine-lives' feline you are,
you could afford to die this once;
but you choose to do otherwise,
'Cus that heart of yours is of a dandelion.

Raising your attractive yellow hair,
you proudly proclaim your triumphs
over the poisons I have always fed to you,
sending a message that's really loud and clear:
That undying heart of yours is of a dandelion.

Faint Whisper

Some days I hear a faint whisper
trying mightily hard to win my trust;
as it plots its dreadful deed.
It's the tenderest I've ever heard.

It blows faintly; barely audible.
I'd swear it's a magic flute;
but knowing from whence it comes,
I refuse to hear its sweet nothings.

Just when it almost convinces me,
to rip my heart in a vengeful act,
a violent blast disrupts its ruse
alerting me to its evil scheme.

We have come a ways o'er time.
Only to sadly reside on opposite ends
due in sum to bruises endured,
which now implore us to evil deeds.

When the Rains Come

There's a struggle between
the sun and the rain.
The dry season is hesitant to leave.
So, it contorts, pouts but to no avail.
Its time has come and gone.

The rains arrive with hidden anger,
disguised beneath a gift of water
for the thirsty, humid and arid land;
luring everyone into false relief.

The dry season watches from a distance,
as it sees the rain drizzle, spates and pour;
muddying the once patched earth
burying it under violent torrents of water.

Soon, reality settles in as all around
the roads become impassable,
waterways begin to overflow,
and zinc dwellings become reservoirs.

Having thought the rain was manna from God,
the people are now left to ponder their fate
as they wait in hopes of the sun's return
while the rain continues to wreak havoc.

Angel

Incandescent,
spellbinding,
unpretending.
These and more you are.
Spiritually and physically, you are
the epitome of all I'd ever desire.

In winds strong or in quiet unperturbed,
you waver not, you retreat not;
you hold on steadfastly, always
trusting our bond, believing in us.

In abundance or in want,
it's never about 'me'; it's always about 'us'.
Unquestioned is your loyalty,
and unsurpassed is your love.

In heaven, when angels are summoned,
of this I am certain
ahead of the line you will be,
unrivaled in your glow.

Beloved In God's Image

My dear beloved
Imagining the speck you were
At the moment of your conception
To the grape you've become today
Confounds me every time
Something magical has happened
In the time that elapsed
Your transformation into
God's glowing image
Has me godsmacked

At the doctor's office the other day
Via the ultrasound, we saw you
Swim in momma's belly;
Like a bubble, you fluttered and floated.
So content you were in that your beautiful world
I could not but marvel at the sight of you
You looked so wholesome in God's image

Soon, we will know for sure
If we'd say 'his' or her' because
You'd be as large as an avocado
Kicking softly in momma's tummy
In God's benevolent image

I wait on you patiently beloved
As you ready to join the family
And make me a proud papa
For what could be the final time

When I see you on arrival,
I'll look you deep in your eyes
To behold God's most reverent image

Midnight Lady

It's only at midnight
    when the spark of the moon
    begins to fade
That she marches up to me
    in all of her tantalizing beauty.

Just when the clock strikes,
    as regular as time,
    she engages me, in my dreams
In a bout of early morning passion
That numbs my senses and dulls reality.

But before I grasped her essence
    just with the wave of her magic wand.
    poof! She disappeared; vanishing into
    thin air as if she was never there.

Oh, you woman of glitter
Ever so fleeting and illusory
Know that in the fullness of time,
Even at your speed of sound,
I'm gonna' find you;
'Cus you're my midnight lady

Could You Be My Mary Anne?

Would you dare try?
To let go of your prejudices?
Of your corrupting stimuli?
To become my 'tried and tested' Mary Anne?

She of sainted memory,
was of a radiant and easy smile,
and interminable goodwill.

Could you even attempt?
To discount my color or race?
Or my accent and religion?
To become my glorious Mary Anne?

She who "saw the worst",
and still 'believed the best",
recognizing none of the identity lines,
that still apportions mankind?

I won't doubt your resolve,
but I'd remind you in earnest,
there was but only one,
of my incomparable Mary Anne.

I am You

Can you not see
That my hue is only skin-deep;
That my accent is man-imposed?
How can you not know
That I am like you?

Since you want to so believe
I will grant you this much:
You may have about you
A little more 'Je ne sais quoi'
But even if it were so
How can you not see,
That I am like you?

Why do you call me names
And throw me shade?
I know my irises are brown
Not blue or green.
Still, aren't you aware
Our blood is colored the same?
Yes, I am you!

Stop the hostility!
And open up to reality
We breathe, sleep and wake
All just the same.
Yes, I am like you.

The Medicine Man

He sits
On a weather-beaten stool
And swivels toward her belly
Which is now fully distended
He has on her a stranglehold

His red, watery eyes wander
First left, then right,
Gazing into hers intently
Intimidating; hypnotizing
He has her now in a near trance

He is ferocious, frightening
So she looks the other way
And that moment he seeks
To convince her of his powers
For he is the medicine man

Aloft he holds a bejeweled cow tail,
Whispering to it magic writs
His fingers dip into a brewing pot
To stir the concoction of deliverance;
He is about to make his claim

Suddenly he 'pulls' a tooth
A leopard's tooth it resembles
"This is from your belly," he says
She shivers; she recoils
With ample fear

Where modern Pharma failed
This mortal succeeds
Gimmickry it may all be
But don't you dare tell her so;
For in this man with the festooned garb,
She places her faith as to life and death

Prophet of Doom

Don't preach to me of gloom
Stressing but the negatives
yet, neglecting the glaring positives.
Have I reminded you lately
that you're a prophet of doom?

I understand you hear fringe society
glorifying your call for expulsion
of people who are different from you;
but may I just remind you
those folks you hate add much to the land,
by their blood and sweat and tears.

I see you feed off the animus thrill
when your extremists pout their hate
fueling you to further insanity;
encouraging you to spew the rage:
the ominous indicators,
the downfall of generations,
the decadence of my people.
Isn't there anything positive,
you, Mr. Prophet of Doom?

No matter how they embolden you,
come the hour of reckoning,
you're bound to fail majorly,
all because you're a prophet of hate.

The Pan-Africanist in Me

I can't stop crying,
trying
to stop the bleeding,
stifling the continent,
of my sacred nativity.

I refuse to stop praying,
hoping
to arrest the larceny,
emptying the coffers,
of my glorious ancestry.

I won't stop seething,
thinking
of the killings,
destroying the gifted progenies,
of my reverent homeland.

Africa, oh my Africa!
What happened to Nkrumah's dreams?
What about Toure's ideals?
Are we heeding Lumumba's pleas?
Or bearing Mandela's torch?

Why are the bulk of our "democracies"
simply tyrannies of minorities?
Designed to foster dynasties,
and enrich corrupt acquaintances?
Why? Africa, Why?

I never will cease reminding,
fighting to awaken the consciences,
of all the "leaders",
neglecting the very well-being,
of my prized but besieged Africa.

Grief

It visits not only when death strikes
one so loved you can't live without,
whisking away a piece of you.
It seizes a heart in other ways too.

The pain of grief is so silent,
it consumes you inside
your head, your heart, your mind—
duping the world of a perfect life.

It pounces not only
where there's a terminal diagnosis,
when the time left to spare
is measured in weeks or months.

That menace called grief
flies like a stealth plane,
piloting silently into a life
it seeks to destroy.

Family, friends and material wealth
are no firewalls
to grief's attack;
it strikes despite the best of them.

When the Mind Soars: Poems from the Heart

Momoh Sekou Dudu

About the Author

Momoh Sekou Dudu comes from the village of Gordorlahun in north-western Liberia. He is the author of the memoir, Harrowing December: Recounting a Journey of Sorrows and Triumphs (201 4); Musings of a Patriot: A Collection of Essays on Liberia (2014), and the forthcoming novel, Forgotten Legacy (2017). He lives in the Minneapolis, Minnesota suburb of Otsego with his wife Mamasu and their two young children: Sekou and Makessa.

Other titles

Harrowing December:
Recounting a Journey of Sorrows and Triumphs (2014)

Musings of a Patriot:
A Collection of Essays on Liberia (2014),

COMING SOON!!!!!!!

Forgotten Legacy (2017)

www.ingramcontent.com/pod-product-compliance
Lightning Source LLC
Chambersburg PA
CBHW071349130626
46556CB00005B/2108